Memorabilia Mixtape

Amanda Giles

BookLeaf
Publishing

India | USA | UK

Presentation by *BookLeaf Publishing*

Web: www.bookleafpub.com

E-mail: info@bookleafpub.com

ISBN: 9789363319295

First edition 2024

For Em, who taught me that the dish could run away with the fork

ACKNOWLEDGEMENT

I extend thanks to my dear ones for encouraging me to share my story through various avenues. My husband, Tony, is a bedrock of support for my creative endeavors. I thank my engaging children for helping me to remain curious as we tandemly grow. I am grateful also to my parents and siblings who helped me to hone my wordsmith skills and to see the world through a lyrical lens. My gratitude also extends to my fellow poets and writerly friends. Each has rendered so much greenhouse care for my seedling thoughts. I have gleaned a wealth of insight from my workshop group: Pacific Wonderland Poets. I also appreciate Jessica Miller for challenging me to write often.

I am privileged to link arms with dedicated school library stewards. We strive to nurture young minds by providing access to story and information. With this in mind, I add my thanks to my magnificent students for sharing their vim and discoveries.

Lastly, I am grateful to BookLeaf Publishing for offering me a springboard from which to high dive.

PREFACE

My early memories play back in my mind as song snatches. This brief book highlights some of the hits and misses at varying tempos. I now loan you my headphones so you can walk a mile in my nostalgic headspace. May you find a way to harmonize with the echoes of my early journey.

Young Life Soundtrack Sampler

Pat-a-caking
Motherese shushing
Lullaby duets

Knee-scrapes
Piano plinks
Transportation ruckus

School bells brrrringing
Autumnal descant
Leaf-crunch stomps

Reverent secrets
Jacket zips
Fresh snow steps

Ping-pong taps
Phone ring-a-linging
Video game beeps

Exuberant Emanation

Massive iridescent spheres
Careen buoyantly
A conglomerate surge
    Lilts and bobs and wends
        Left to right across the riverfront
Born of stringed sticks
Doused and pulled
Finessed and eked
Via delicate dedication
From a lone bubble mother
    Elevated upon a platform box
        To direct each measure
           Of this visual symphony
Bulbous whole notes dance across an invisible staff
    Underscored by the lapping of the current
        Against buoys and the silty river edge
This solitary bubble farmer sows with repetitive commitment
Reaping more whimsy than lazy Mondays tend to generate
    The courier wind accepts each fleeting liquid offering
        Disseminating orbs as they glimmer
           And rotate into the periwinkle
              Onward into the effervescing hearts
              Of each watchful bubble gleaner

Supermarket Interview

That tall, tall man
Bent low, low, low to ask if
I loved my baby doll
Just like Mom loved you

"Of course I do!"

He then wondered aloud
About whether or not
I rocked my baby doll
When Mom rocked you

"Of course I do!"

He cast one last query
Hoping to discover if
I fed my baby doll
Just like Mom fed you

"Of course not! My belly buttons aren't big enough yet!"

Cardboard House Party

A gilded memory whirs unbidden
A fractured filmstrip
Reclaimed from life's cutting room floor
I am 4 and you are 2

We giggle on our blanket-carpet
Nestled safely in the mini-dwelling
Engineered by our father—
A welcoming escape
From the pressures of tot-hood

A light thap-thap-thap
At the corrugated door—

We peek through Exacto-cut windows
To discover beaming Mom—with sippy cups
And a tray of young-palette charcuterie:
Cheese
Peanut butter
Saltines
Grapes

Our nook's octagonal base showcases
Marker-scrawled daisies and tulips
Stick figure portraits adorn the inner walls
We host our stuffed animals
Owning this shared place
Cementing our sisterhood

The greatest bonus from Dad's grocery era?
This watermelon box for two

Midday Silver Lining

At high noon
We giggle-race
From horsey swings
To the ladder scramble
We breath-catch
After pinnacling
The sizzle slide
Our achievement
So lofty that Mom
Ceases talking to the
Other bench moms
Shielding her eyes
To wince-witness
Our brash descent
You hover your feet
To spare your legs
From the sheet pan chute
That would bake you into
A gingerbread girl
I mimic your posture
And glide to meet you
Again, again, again
Until the thrill fades
Into dozy dreams
As we nap-slide through
The car ride home

Tonka Truck Tanka

Mighty canary
Paint-chipped as a chewn pencil
Trusty dune shifter

Mound-surrounded steel monarch
Stalwart sandboxed behemoth

Was it Brittani?

I cannot recall the name of that brazen
neighborhood menace. A roiling tar pit
burbled in her small-girl soul. Had a
cruelty guide apprenticed her? Did she
brim her own inner vessel with pitch and
spite, or had others filled and hung the vat
above her ever-stoked fire of contempt?
Hardship somehow folly-fueled her to
Pithily provoke you to attempt this feat.

She rightly sized you up. An indefatigable
iceberg in her way: dauntless, courageous.
Sparked by jealousy, her firecracker fuse
sizzled into a dare. She challenged you
to traverse the griddle-hot hood of her father's
bronze sedan on the white hottest Hades day.

I was not witness to The Event, but my mind
constructed a visceral semblance of the scene.
Your dismount from the nearest branch is
executed flawlessly. You strut confidently—
eyebrows held aloft by prowess-awareness
and hubris. You register danger after damage
is severe. Your smug smile flash-melts into
warped grimace. You hop, drop, and roll
like an upturned beetle on the grassy verge.

I do recall your whimper cries as Dad cradled
you and your courage while Mom replaced the salve
and bandages. Phoenix-fire shimmered in your eyes.
Is your oppressor's name seared as a memory scar
Melded with the scorch-sounds of betrayal and
The weeping of your blistered small-girl feet?

Hoppy Taw

I lower on flamingo leg
To retrieve my hopscotch marker
From number seven
I pogo my way through the final jumps
And reclaim my place in the queue
Your toss to eight lands on the line
You dejectedly reclaim it
Stomping your discontent

Lisa J. lobs her disc cleanly to ten
And buoyantly begins the course
I swallow and halt my breath
Unsure if I should cheer for success
Or if it would be evil to pray
That she might just possibly bobble

She triumphs and closes this round
With an overhead flex

We collect our respective colorful discs
Our names etched on the edges
With permanent marker commitment
We hopscotch home on phantom frames
Calling:

HOP–eee–TAAAW
HOP–eee–TAAAW
HOP–eee–TAAAW

Backyard Focal Point

Each recycled summer
We'd watch—impatient

Buds and blossoms
Morphed our climbing tree
Into a popcorn pom-pom tree
Resplendent at the golden hour

Petal-fall signaled
Impending miracle

Our eyes dilated
At the staggered growth
And ripening hue
Of each ellipsoid
Chartreusing
Into a velveted
Blushed coral

Finally inviting us
To harvest
Stone fruit promises
Juicy chins
Tummy aches
Chores for children

We had not fully grasped
That we were also growing

Our aunts surely noticed
And said so to our mother
Who was sizing up our cousins
At the family reunion
Where our giant metal bowl

Proferred apricot perfection
From our philanthropic tree

Chauffered by Spontaneity

Hey! Remember how Mom
   took zany side-quest routes
      after the erranding was done?
         At long stoplights
            she decreed that we must
               hastily seat-swap.
The exhilaration
   of exiting the car
      racing and re-buckling
         just ahead of the green light.
            Our heartbeats downshifted through
               staggered laugh-breaths.
A solitary, stoic passenger
   was exempt from the shuffle.
      Our imaginary travel companion—
         a mostly invisible leopard—Murphy
            As steadfast as his purple spots
               Maintained his center console position.

Ronde in the Reeds

Gilded rays filter down to the buzzing below
While red-winged blackbirds exchange homing calls
Lemony irises protect the pond in a circling sway
Widgeons huddle-swim to peep and plash

While red-winged blackbirds exchange homing calls
A heron wends nestward through the blue
Widgeons huddle-swim to peep and plash
A dragonfly navigates spindly rushes

A heron wends nestward through the blue
Gilded rays filter down to the buzzing below
A dragonfly navigates spindly rushes
Lemony irises protect the pond in a circling sway

Skipportunity

The mega jump-rope
Undulates as it is tugged
Across the blacktop
This oversized macaroni necklace
Rainbows upward into full sway
Pulled taut by two rope-twirling heroes

Synchronized arms
Swoop the cord high
Thwap it back down
Regulating the pace
As if with a metronome

I head-bob to the rhythm
Gulp a bravery breath
Lean in
Leap in
All in

The staccato slaps of my Keds
Add syncopated percussion
To this intricate recess dance
Twenty-three . . .
Twenty-four . . .
Twenty-five . . .

Lunar Surface

Butter-churned moon, one day from full
Escapes the eclipse of a range of conifer tips
Beaming from azure backdrop of early evening

This languid moon, low and oversized
Tracks our trajectory with deep-set vigilance
Offering pleasant, lambent approval

"Look! The moon is smiling!"

"I don't even see a face."

We double back to crane for a clearer view
I point-trace the key features
Highlighting brow, sockets, nose line, generous grin

"Do you see it now?"

Steady head shake
Graduated smile-break
Power shrug

"I really have no wish to find the face. I want the moon to
simply be the moon."

Glee for Me and a Bother to my Father

I informed you of my plans to go
Were you truly surprised
That I sneaked out?

Consumed wholly
I had been abuzz for days
After receiving word

A blockbuster movie
With explosions–and a car chase–and two A-list actors
To be filmed just blocks from our house?!

Wearing jeans and a tee
I waited you out–tucked under the covers
Amassing hope and moxie

You switched off the hall light
Triggering a 17-minute cushioning pause
Then I donned my quietest shoes

Suppressed steps across carpet and tile
10-inched me closer to the sliding door
I laboriously closed the minimal gap behind me

Conjuring wall-scaling dauntlessness
I stealth-clambered the stucco perimeter
With negligible hand damage

Floodlights beckoned like a sunrise
As I ratcheted into sprint mode
With the vigor of an Olympic hopeful

I ranged through the milling congregation
Scouring for the friend who keenly knew
I WOULD NOT be coming meant I SURELY WOULD

I conquered this second, taller wall
Squeezing into a gap between gawkers
Landing like a crow on an overcrowded wire

As my breathing steadied
I relished the wondrous splendor
Of all the lights, all the cameras, all the action

The facades of the row houses yet to be built
Looked comical from behind the filming zone
My soul dilated at the gift of this backstage pass

Cars raced through the short housing tract
For pass after pass—take after take
I squint-scanned for a glimpse of the superstars

My circulation had slackened
The desert wind pricked my neck and ears
I noticed my buddy's jacket and shivered

She handed me her thermos of cocoa
And I sipped gratefully then choked
At the sound of a blaring, familiar horn

You trumpeted your signature honk pattern
Inconceivably, you had located me
Among that beaded string of perched people

My cheeks bloomed fresh racing stripes
And I hunched down, yearn-willing my own invisibility
The syncopated honking persisted, so I turned

You peered upward through the car window
Bidding my descent

With that parental finger curl

For a moment, I entertained a pivot-plan
Of hopping off the front of the high wall
Surely to join the production team as an extra

But I skidded down against the grating wall
And my own mortifying defeat
To this car ride home and weighty consequence

You grumble-grounded me for 6 weeks
After I tearfully spluttered: "Worth it!"
When Mom cooed for clemency, you settled on a month

Four weeks later, my hot cocoa friend reported:
"I never saw the movie stars, but you missed the explosions!"
Not the one from my dad, I thought

Ready!

Our make-up caddies flank the sink
In synchrony we lean toward the mirror
For one last application of mascara
Each mouth agape in an awkward oval

Tunes we blast for gussying
Buzz against the countertop
The shoulder strap of the pale pink boombox
Droops over the open drawer

We duet into our hairbrushes
Then tease our locks vigorously
Defying gravity and good sense
And the scorn of older generations

The fffft of the hairspray zings
Over your shoulder into my eye
Eliciting a primal yowl
With reflexive elbow jab

I rinse and reinsert my contact lens
And rectify mascara's mayhem
We nod our mutual forgiveness
Seal it with a crisp high five

Tandem application of metallic gloss
Forms icing on this pregame ritual
Highlighting the shine in our Saturday eyes
We unplug the curling iron and dance out the door

Arpeggio Season

Reinitiation
Celebration of fresh clay
Choreographed into position
Lifeblood and heartbeat
Festooned with vines
That certain promising green
Backlit by the sun
Dandelion seeds skydive
Daydreams effervesce
Into budding emergence
Youthful curiosity traces
Innumerable raindrop races
Zigging down the dappled
Picture window
Into thirsty daffodillies

Kiln Season

The satisfying kindness
Of a shared twin popsicle
After a trampoline morning
Blaring anthems
Bursting with berries and cherries
The glass-blown grill marks
Of freckles and sunburn
Rolling down the rolling hills
Watermelon seeds propelled
Watermelon juice chin-traveling
Languid, vivid, humid
Tomato plants in terra-cotta nests
Jewel-toned carousel tunes
Balancing the heat-warped streets
With spiraling clinks of ice
In a lemonade glass

Nutmeg Season

Jumbo erasers
Sharpened pencils ready
Chilled walks through cheeky wind
Welcoming reprieve
On a leaf mattress
Canopied by rusted broadleaves
Galloping home
To the kitchen glow
Roasted pumpkin seeds
Delicate garnish atop
Butternut squash soup
In a generous, russet bowl
Paired with the big spoon
Warmth blooms outward
Spooky stories offer
Bravery practice
Wrapped in a light quilt

Cocoon Season

Insulated reflection
Scarf-encircled souls
Nestled in parka stuffing
Toes frosted, thawed, toasted—on loop
Ideas frosted, thawed, toasted—on loop
All swaddled in softest socks
While whipped cream peaks
Jag across the horizon
And bob atop steaming cocoa
Fireglow dances across
The final layer of pottery glaze
This loyal mug harbors
Every sweetness of an entire year

Childhoodwinked

The looking glass of decades gone
Somehow merges my two silhouettes
Rosy vellum of some youthful version
Aligns with the outline of today me
I embody this amalgamation of self
My inner construction paper heart
Still reverberates wonderment
Conversations with characters
Papercut scars from books
Healed by kinship with fiction
Hand cramps from game controllers
Tempered by the freedom of commercial breaks
Interluded by intertwinings of park days and movie nights
Vinyl spinning at the right RPM and the wrong RPM
Spiraling belief that rebellion is unacceptable
Attestation that rebellion is essential
My interloping smartphone seeks to supersede
Partially eclipsing all prior influences
Indignation swirls with nostalgia
Rewinding my mixtape with a beveled ballpoint
Motley memories strum against my heartstrings
Embodying bittersweet vacillation
Insular solitude of headphones and Walkman
Crescendos build to boomboxed camaraderie

Solstice Wingspan

24

Sunbright swaths unfurl
Taffy-tugging the warmed day
Toward full moonglow

Cricket thwerps pulse a rhythm
Sibilant wind-whisper lulls